Flyers

Rebecca Rissman

raintree

a Capstone company — publishers for children

Raintree is an imprint of Capstone Global Library Limited, a company incorporated in England and Wales having its registered office at 7 Pilgrim Street, London, EC4V 6LB – Registered company number: 6695582

www.raintreepublishers.co.uk
myorders@raintreepublishers.co.uk

Text © Capstone Global Library Limited 2015
First published in hardback in 2014
First published in paperback in 2015
The moral rights of the proprietor have been asserted.

Edited by Brynn Baker, Clare Lewis, and
        Helen Cox Cannons
Designed by Kyle Grenz and Tim Bond
Picture research by Tracy Cummins
Production by Helen McCreath
Originated by Capstone Global Library Limited
Printed and bound in China by Leo Paper Group

ISBN 978-1-406-28280-1 (hardback)
18 17 16 15 14
10 9 8 7 6 5 4 3 2 1

ISBN 978-1-406-28287-0 (paperback)
19 18 17 16 15
10 9 8 7 6 5 4 3 2 1

British Library Cataloguing in Publication Data
A full catalogue record for this book is available from the British Library.

Acknowledgements
We would like to thank the following for permission to reproduce photographs: Ardea: © Yves Bilat, 6, 23f; FLPA: Christian Ziegler/Minden Pictures, 11, Claus Meyer/Minden Pictures, 19, Derek Middleton, 7 mouse, Emanuele Biggi, 9, 23h, Hugh Clark, 21, front cover, Hugh Lansdown, 17, 23e, Imagebroker, 7 owl, Michael Durham/Minden Pictures, 13, 18, 22, back cover, Michael Mayer, 20, Michel Rauch/Biosphoto, 4, 10, 23d, Roger Tidman, 16, 23c; Getty Images: Auscape/UIG, 12, 23b, Fred Bruemmer, 15, James Hager, 5, Les Stocker, 14; Shutterstock: Andrew Astbury, 7 fox, Piotr Krzeslak, 7 hedgehog.

Every effort has been made to contact copyright holders of material reproduced in this book. Any omissions will be rectified in subsequent printings if notice is given to the publisher.

Contents

What is a bat?

A bat is a small, flying **mammal**. It has large ears, small eyes, and sharp teeth.

Bats have long arms attached to their leathery wings for support.

Bats are rarely seen during the day.
This is because they are **nocturnal**.

What does nocturnal mean?

Nocturnal means awake during the night.

Animals that are nocturnal sleep during the day.

fox

owl

hedgehog

mouse

Many animals are nocturnal.

Foxes, owls, hedgehogs, and mice are nocturnal.

Where do bats live?

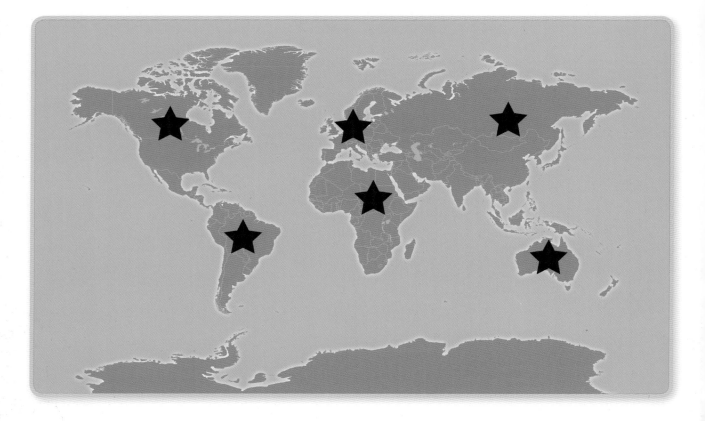

Bats live on every **continent** except for Antarctica.

They live in groups called colonies.

Bats spend days sleeping in dark, quiet places called **roosts**.

Roosts can be found in caves, holes in trees, and even in some attics!

What do bats eat?

Different types of bats eat different foods.

Most bats eat small insects, such as moths, beetles, and flies.

Many bats eat pests, such as mosquitos. Some bats eat fruit.

Some bats even drink the blood of other animals!

How do bats find prey?

Most bats look for food at night when it is dark outside.

Some bats use **echolocation** to find food to eat.

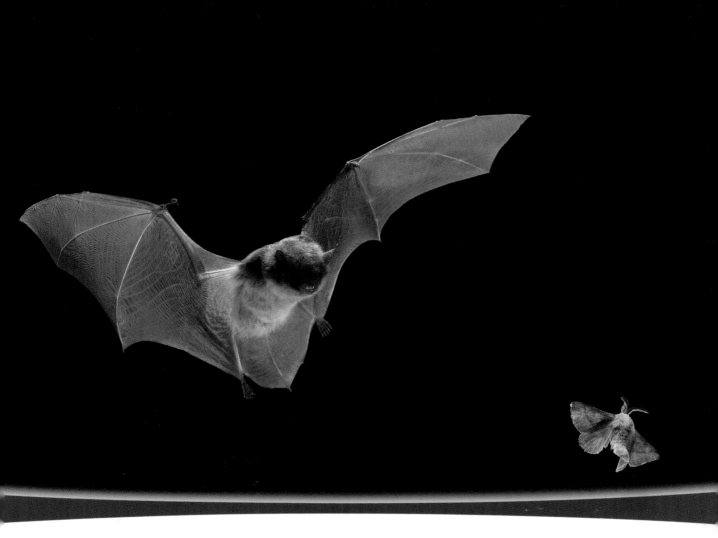

Bats make noises and listen for echoes.

Their sensitive ears tell them where food can be found.

What are bat babies like?

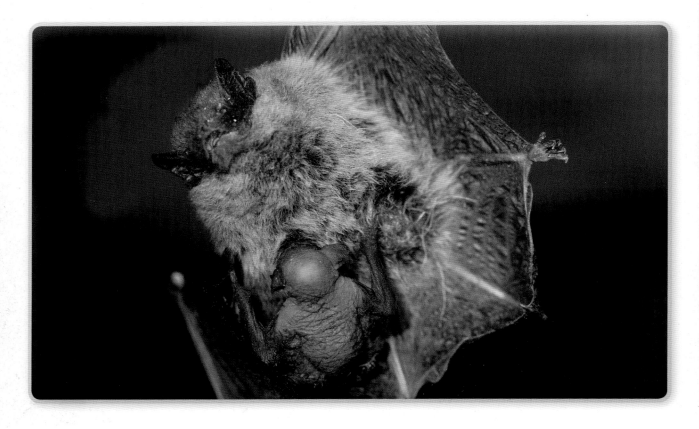

Each year, female bats give birth to one or two babies called pups.

The pups are hairless and very small.

Female bats care for their pups for about one month.

Then the young bats fly off by themselves.

Where do bats go in winter?

Many bats **hibernate** during winter.

They sleep in a safe, warm place
until spring.

Other bats **migrate**.

They fly to warmer places during winter and return to their homes every spring.

How can you spot bats?

Bats are most active one or two hours after the Sun sets.

Some of the most common places bats live are in caves or tree hollows.

Bats do not fly in smooth lines like most birds. Bats fly in jerky zigzags.

Watch the skies carefully for small animals making twists and turns.

How can you help bats?

Avoid using sprays to poison pests.

They make it hard for bats to find food.

Never touch bats. Some bats carry diseases that can make you ill.

If you see a bat, tell a trusted adult.

Bat body map

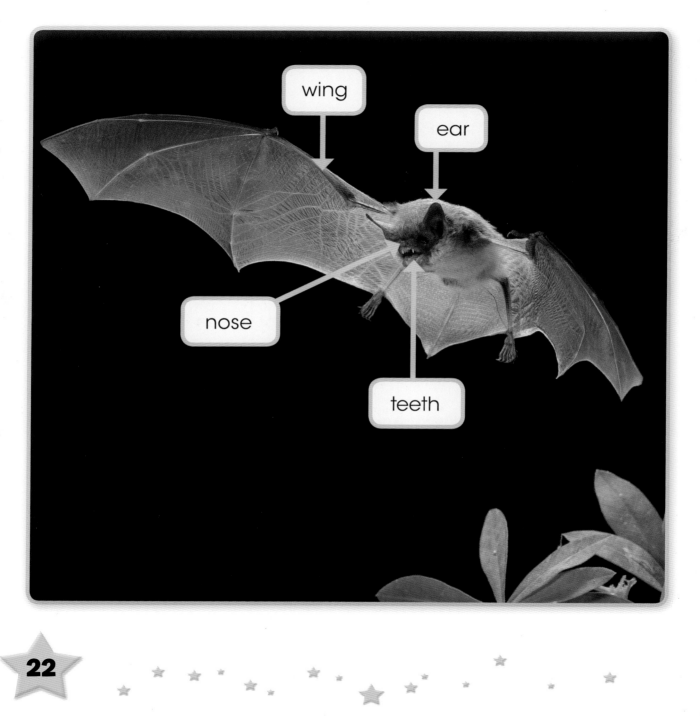

wing

ear

nose

teeth

Picture glossary

 **continent** one of seven huge areas of land on Earth

 **echolocation** the use of sound vibrations for navigation

 **hibernate** to spend the winter in a deep sleep

 **mammal** warm-blooded animal that has a back-bone, hair or fur, and gives birth to live babies that feed on milk from the mother

 **migrate** when an animal moves from one area to another because of the seasons

 **nocturnal** awake at night and asleep during the day

 **roost** quiet, dark place bats gather and sleep

Find out more

Books

Bat (British Animals), Stephen Savage (Wayland, 2012)

Bats (Nocturnal Animals), J. Angelique Johnson (Capstone Press, 2011)

Websites

Discover more about bat conservation and research at:
www.bats.org.uk

Learn more bat facts at:
www.bbc.co.uk/nature/life/Bat

Index